All Moms
Should Have 4 Hands

R-R-I-I-N-N-G-G

Crispo

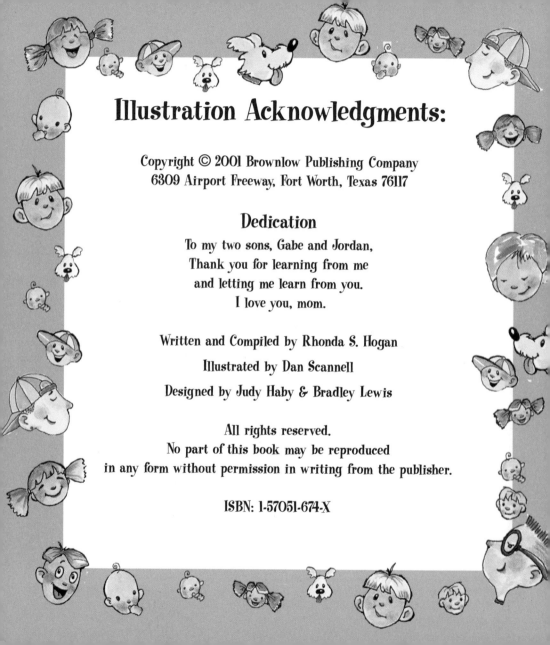

Illustration Acknowledgments:

Copyright © 2001 Brownlow Publishing Company
6309 Airport Freeway, Fort Worth, Texas 76117

Dedication

To my two sons, Gabe and Jordan,
Thank you for learning from me
and letting me learn from you.
I love you, mom.

Written and Compiled by Rhonda S. Hogan

Illustrated by Dan Scannell

Designed by Judy Haby & Bradley Lewis

ISBN: 1-57051-674-X

Presented To

_____

By

_____

_____

_____

Date

Table of Contents

All Moms Should Have 4 Hands

R-R-I-I-N-N-G-G

Crispo

Brownlow

Written by
Rhonda S. Hogan

Illustrated by
Dan Scannell

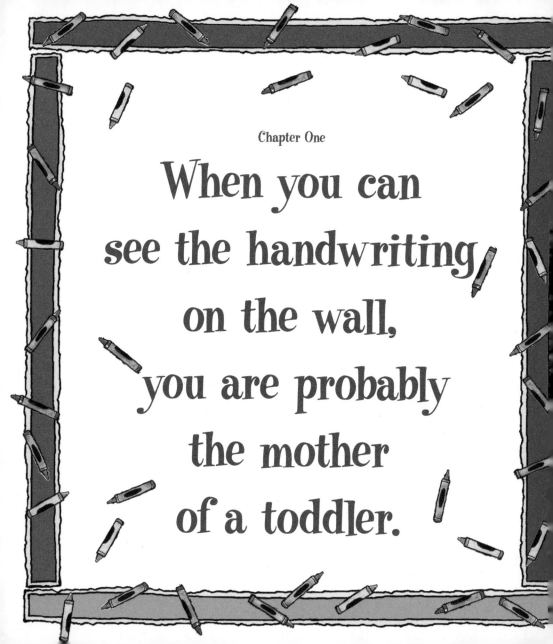

Chapter One

When you can see the handwriting on the wall, you are probably the mother of a toddler.

There is no slave out of heaven like a loving woman;
and of all loving women, there is no slave as a mother.

Henry Ward Beecher

A man's work is from sun to sun,
But a mother's work is never done.

Anonymous

She also rises while it is yet night,
and provides food for your household,
and a portion for her maidens.

Proverbs 31:15

The most important handshake of your life
will happen when your newborn infant's tiny hand
grabs hold of your index finger.

Anonymous

Every child born into this world is a new thought of God,
an ever-fresh and radiant possibility.

Kate Douglas Wiggin

This house has a protective shield—dust.

No matter how old a mother is, she watches
her middle-aged children for signs of improvement.

Florida Scott Maxwell

A young boy was served canned corn for dinner.
Looking up hopefully, he advised his mother,
"I really would like it better on a "roller.""

Housewife's Lament

Make the beds, bandage heads,
Straighten up the room;
Wash the windows, cut the grass,
See the tulips bloom.

Drive the children to school,
Drive them back again.
Have the Cubs to meeting
Then I clean the den.

Serve on my committee,
Attend the P.T.A.
Forgot to buy the children shoes...
Can't do it today.

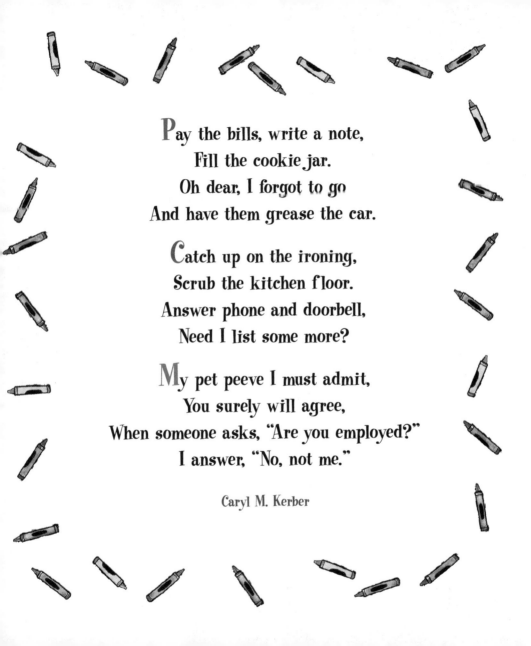

Pay the bills, write a note,
Fill the cookie jar.
Oh dear, I forgot to go
And have them grease the car.

Catch up on the ironing,
Scrub the kitchen floor.
Answer phone and doorbell,
Need I list some more?

My pet peeve I must admit,
You surely will agree,
When someone asks, "Are you employed?"
I answer, "No, not me."

Caryl M. Kerber

Chapter Two

Daily Workouts

You know you are a mom when your daily workout consists of getting up at 5:30 am and staying up each night until midnight bathing, brushing, buckling, budgeting, changing sheets, changing diapers, chasing, clipping coupons, cooking, dragging out of bed, driving, drying, dusting, feeding (them, not you), flushing, folding clothes, helping with homework, ironing, loading, unloading, shopping, sweeping, paying bills, picking up, putting to bed, vacuuming, washing, wiping, PLUS basketball, bike riding, bubbles, catch, cuddling, dolls, coloring, crafts, football, jumping rope, nature walks, playing baseball, pushing trucks, roller-blading, slides, sprinklers, swinging, PLUS edging, gardening, mowing, painting, planting, raking, trimming, and walking the dog. You have no time to eat, sleep, drink, or go to the bathroom, and yet— you still managed to gain ten pounds!

For the mother is and must be, whether she knows it or not, the greatest, strongest, and most lasting teacher her children have.

Hannah Whitall Smith

■

It takes a hundred men to make an encampment, but one woman can make a home.

Robert G. Ingerson

■

To love children is to love God.

Roy Rogers

■

You can be sure of two things in this world: There is a God and your mother loves you.

Rhonda S. Hogan

■

There are three ways to get something done—do it yourself, hire someone to do it, or ask your kids not to do it.

Malcolm Kushner

It is the wise parent who gives his child
roots and wings.

Chinese Proverb

Separation anxiety happens to babies at nine
months; to mothers their whole lives.

Good Question??

A ten-year old boy left the table without
finishing the wonderful lunch his mother
had prepared for him. In exasperation
she asked, "How could you leave so much
of your food untouched? Don't you know
millions of people around the world are
starving to death?"
The boy promptly replied, "Name two!"

Chapter Three

◆

The Meanest Mother

◆

I had the meanest mother in the whole world. While other kids
ate candy for breakfast, I had to have cereal, eggs, or toast.
When others had cokes and candy for lunch, I had to eat a sandwich.
As you can guess, my supper was different from the other kids' too.
But at least I wasn't alone in my sufferings. My siblings had
the same mean mother as I did.

My mother insisted upon knowing where we were at all times.
You'd think we were on a chain gang. She had to know who
our friends were and what we were doing. She insisted
if we said we'd be gone an hour that we be gone one hour or less–not
one hour and one minute.

The worst is yet to come. We had to be in bed by nine each night
and up early the next morning. We couldn't even sleep till noon
like our friends. So while they slept, my mother actually had the nerve
to break the child labor law. She made us work. We had to wash dishes,
make beds, learn to cook, and all sorts of cruel things.
I believe she laid awake at night thinking up mean things to do to us.

She always insisted upon our telling the truth, the whole truth, and nothing but the truth, even if it killed us–it nearly did.

By the time we were teenagers, she was much wiser, and our life became even more unbearable. None of this tooting the horn of a car for us to come running. She embarrassed us to no end by making our dates and friends come to the door to get us. I forgot to mention that while my friends were dating at the mature age of 12 and 13, my old-fashioned mother refused to let me date until the age of 15 and 16. Fifteen, that is, if you dated only to go to a school function, and that was once or twice a year.

My mother was a complete failure as a mother. None of us has ever been arrested, divorced, or beat his mate. Whom do we have to blame for the terrible way we turned out? You're right, our mean mother. Look at all the things we missed!

We never got to march in a protest parade, nor take part in a riot, burn draft cards, and a million and one things that our friends did.

She forced us to grow up into God-fearing, educated, honest adults. Using this as a background, I am trying to raise my children. I stand a little taller and I am filled with pride when my children call me mean. Because, you see, I thank God. He gave me the meanest mother in the whole world.

Anonymous

Moms do have four hands–or all the hands that they need–when they depend on God. As mothers, we may have two physical hands, but through God we are given the extra hands we need to care for our kids. Just try to not depend on God and you will find that even the two hands you have are not enough!

Rhonda S. Hogan

Unless the Lord builds the house, they labor in vain who build it; unless the Lord guards the city, the watchman stays awake in vain.

Psalm 127:1 (NKJV)

Little boy to his mother: "Before I tell you what happened, Mom, remember the Lord will never give you more than you can handle."

Working Mothers

A mother works and works and works.
And the willingness with which she does it
is the chief contribution to a pleasant
and happy family.

It has been said that the thrush goes to work
at half-past two every morning during the summer
and works until nine-thirty at night—
a straight nineteen hours—during which it feeds
its young over two hundred times.

The blackbird works seventeen hours
and feeds its little ones a hundred times a day.

In the home the energetic mother is up early
and retires late. Like the hard-working bird,
she does it for those who are so precious to her.

Leroy Brownlow,
Today is Mine

Wild Sunflowers And Mother

Out in the meadow, I picked a wild sunflower,
and as I looked into its golden heart, such a wave
of homesickness came over me that I almost wept.
I wanted Mother, with her gentle voice and quiet firmness;
I longed to hear Father's jolly songs and to see his twinkling
blue eyes; I was lonesome for the sister with whom
I used to play in the meadow picking daisies
and wild sunflowers.

Across the years, the old home and its love called to me,
and memories of sweet words of counsel came flooding back.
I realize that all my life the teachings of those early
days have influenced me, and the example set by Father and
Mother has been something I have tried to follow, with failures
here and there, with rebellion at times; but always coming
back to it as the compass needle to the star.

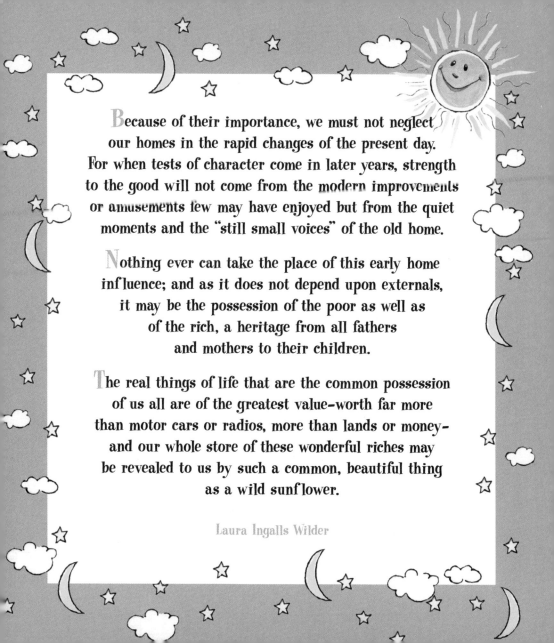

Because of their importance, we must not neglect
our homes in the rapid changes of the present day.
For when tests of character come in later years, strength
to the good will not come from the modern improvements
or amusements few may have enjoyed but from the quiet
moments and the "still small voices" of the old home.

Nothing ever can take the place of this early home
influence; and as it does not depend upon externals,
it may be the possession of the poor as well as
of the rich, a heritage from all fathers
and mothers to their children.

The real things of life that are the common possession
of us all are of the greatest value–worth far more
than motor cars or radios, more than lands or money–
and our whole store of these wonderful riches may
be revealed to us by such a common, beautiful thing
as a wild sunflower.

Laura Ingalls Wilder

Chapter Four

To Preserve Children

Take one large grassy field,
one-half dozen children, two or three
small dogs, a pinch of brook,
and some pebbles. Mix the children
and dogs well together and put them
in the field, stirring constantly.
Pour the brook over the pebbles;
sprinkle the field with flowers;
spread over all a deep blue sky,
and bake in the hot sun. When brown,
remove and set to cool in the bathtub.

Rhonda S. Hogan

A Parable for Mothers

The young mother set her foot on the path of life. "Is the way long?" she asked. And her guide said, "Yes. And the way is hard. And you will be old before you reach the end of it. But the end will be better than the beginning." But the young mother was happy, and she would not believe that anything could be better than these years. So she played with her children, and gathered flowers for them along the way, and bathed with them in the clear streams; and the sun shone on them, and life was good, and the young mother cried, "Nothing will ever be lovelier than this."

Then night came, and a storm, and the path was dark, and the children shook with fear and cold, and the mother drew them close and covered them with her mantle, and the children said, "Oh, Mother, we are not afraid, for you are near, and no harm can come." And the mother said, "This is better than the brightness of day, for I have taught my children courage."

And the morning came, and there was a hill ahead, and the children climbed and grew weary, and the mother was weary, but at all times she said to the children, "A little patience, and we are there." So the children climbed, and when they reached the top, they said, "We could not have done it without you, Mother."

And the mother, when she lay down that night, looked up at the stars, and said, "This is a better day than the last, for my children have learned fortitude in the face of hardness. Yesterday I gave them courage. Today I have given them strength."

And the next day came strange clouds, which darkened the earth–clouds of war and hate and evil, and the children groped and stumbled, and the mother said, "Look up. Lift your eyes to the Light."

And the children looked and saw above the clouds an Everlasting Glory, and it guided them and brought them beyond the darkness. And that night the mother said, "This is the best day of all, for I have shown my children God."

And the days went on, and the weeks and the months and the years, and the mother grew old, and she was little and bent. But her children were tall and strong, and walked with courage. And when the way was hard, they helped their mother; and when the way was rough, they lifted her, for she was as light as a feather; and at last they came to a hill, and beyond the hill they could see a shining road and golden gates flung wide. And the mother said, "I have reached the end of my journey. And now I know that the end is better than the beginning, for my children can walk alone, and their children after them."

And the children said, "You will always walk with us, Mother, even when you have gone through the gates." And they stood and watched her as she went on alone, and the gates closed after her. And they said, "We cannot see her, but she is with us still. A mother like ours is more than a memory. She is a living presence."

Author Unknown

A pediatrician was once asked
by a mother what was the best time
to put her children to bed. He replied,
"While you still have the strength."

In a crowded mall a little boy lost his mother.
He went in and out of stores and saw women
carrying packages, but none was his mother.
He finally found a security guard and, pointing
to the passing crowd, asked, "Mister, did you
happen to see a woman going by without me?"

A Mother's Prayer

Lord, give me patience when wee hands
Tug at me with their small demands.
Give me gentle and smiling eyes;
Keep my lips from hasty replies.
Let not weariness, confusion, or noise
Obscure my vision of life's fleeting joys.
So, when in years to come, my house is still–
No bitter memories its rooms may fill.

Our efforts to train our children are never wasted. Sooner or later they will come around.

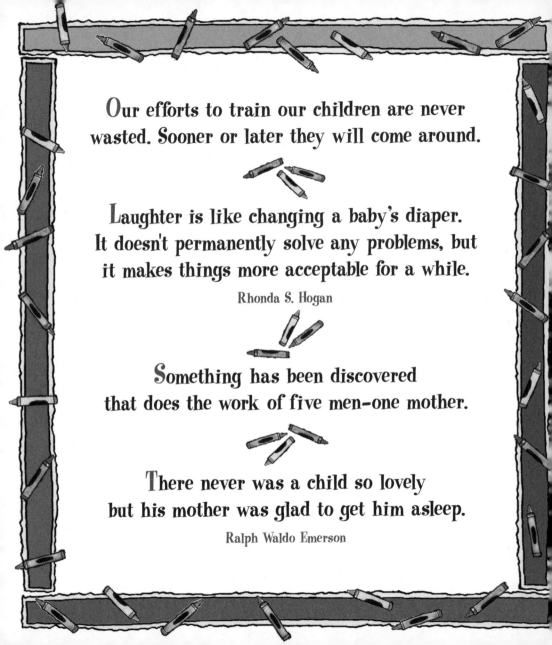

Laughter is like changing a baby's diaper. It doesn't permanently solve any problems, but it makes things more acceptable for a while.

Rhonda S. Hogan

Something has been discovered that does the work of five men—one mother.

There never was a child so lovely but his mother was glad to get him asleep.

Ralph Waldo Emerson

You know you're a mom when...

- Popsicles become a food staple.

- Your feet stick to the kitchen floor...
    and you don't care.

- You can't find your cordless phone, so you ask
    a friend to call you, and you run around the house
    madly, following the sound until you locate
    the phone downstairs in the laundry basket.

- Your baby's pacifier falls on the floor and you give
    it back to her, after you suck the dirt off of it
    because your too busy to wash it off.

- The closest you get to gourmet cooking is making
    Rice Crispy bars.

Chapter Five

Wet Oatmeal Kisses

■

One of these days you'll explode and shout to all the kids,
"Why don't you just grow up and act your age!"
And they will.

■

Or, 'You guys get outside and find something to do-
without hurting each other and don't slam the door!"
And they don't.

■

You'll straighten their bedrooms until it's all neat and tidy,
toys displayed on the shelf, hangers in the closet, animals
caged. You'll yell, "Now I want it to stay this way!"
And it will.

■

You will prepare a perfect dinner with a salad that
hasn't had all the olives picked out and a cake
with no finger traces in the icing and you'll say,
"Now this is a meal for company."
And you will eat it alone.

■

You'll yell, "I want complete privacy on the phone.
No screaming, do you hear me?"
And no one will answer.

No more plastic tablecloths stained, no more dandelion
bouquets. No more iron-on patches, no more wet, knotted
shoelaces, muddy boots, or rubber bands for ponytails.
Imagine—a lipstick with a point, no babysitters
for New Years Eve, washing clothes only once a week, no PTA
meetings or silly school plays where your child is a tree,
no car pools, blaring stereos, or forgotten lunch money.
No more Christmas presents made of library paste
and toothpicks, no wet oatmeal kisses, no more tooth fairy,
no more giggles in the dark, scraped knees to kiss
or sticky fingers to clean.
Only a voice asking, "Why don't you grow up?"
And the silence echoes: "I did."

Author Unknown

Father asked us what was God's noblest work.
Anna said men, but I said babies.
Men are often bad; babies never are.
Louisa May Alcott

Everyone is in awe of the lion tamer in a cage
with half a dozen lions–everyone but a mother.

We find delight in the beauty and happiness
of children that makes the heart too big for the body.
Ralph Waldo Emerson

Children need love, especially when
they do not deserve it.
Harold Hulbert

Train Him Well

A child is a person who is going to carry
on what you have started. He is going to sit where
you are sitting, and when you are gone attend
to those things which you think are important.
You may adopt all the policies you please, but how
they are carried out depends on him. He will assume
control of your cities, states, and nations. He is going
to move in and take over your churches, schools,
universities, and corporations–the fate of our nations is
in his hands–so train him well.

Abraham Lincoln

 # Little Eyes

There are little eyes upon you
And they're watching night and day.
There are little ears that quickly
Take in every word you say.

There are little hands all eager
To do anything you do;
And little children dreaming
Of the day they'll be like you.

They believe in you devoutly,
Hold all you say and do,
They will say and do, in your way
When they're grown up just like you.

There's a wide-eyed little student
Who believes you're always right;
And their eyes are always open,
And they watch you day and night.

You are setting an example
Every day in all you do;
For the little child who's waiting
To grow up to be like you.

Anonymous

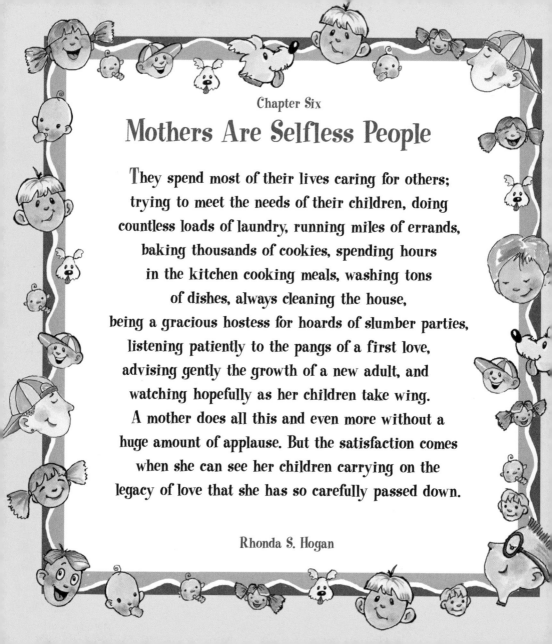

Chapter Six

Mothers Are Selfless People

They spend most of their lives caring for others;
trying to meet the needs of their children, doing
countless loads of laundry, running miles of errands,
baking thousands of cookies, spending hours
in the kitchen cooking meals, washing tons
of dishes, always cleaning the house,
being a gracious hostess for hoards of slumber parties,
listening patiently to the pangs of a first love,
advising gently the growth of a new adult, and
watching hopefully as her children take wing.
A mother does all this and even more without a
huge amount of applause. But the satisfaction comes
when she can see her children carrying on the
legacy of love that she has so carefully passed down.

Rhonda S. Hogan

A mother is not a person to lean on but a person
to make leaning unnecessary.

Dorothy Canfield Fisher

Parents are people who bear children, bore teenagers,
and board newlyweds.

Anonymous

Mothers spend half their time wondering how their children will
turn out and the other half wondering when they will turn in.

Rhonda S. Hogan

A mother is someone who dreams great dreams for you,
but then she lets you chase the dreams you have
for yourself and loves you just the same.

Anonymous

We leave traces of ourselves wherever
we go, on whatever we touch.

Lewis Thomas

A mother is the one who is still there
when everyone else has deserted you.

Anonymous

A cheerful look brings joy to the heart.
Proverbs 15:30

A small house will hold as much happiness
as a big one.
Anonymous

The greatest work that you will ever do
will be within the four walls of your home.

Where your pleasure is,
there is your treasure.
Where your treasure is, there is
your heart. Where your heart is,
there is your happiness.
Augustine

Chapter Seven

Real Mothers

Real Mothers don't eat quiche; they don't have time to make it.

Real Mothers know that their kitchen utensils are probably
in the sandbox.

Real Mothers often have sticky floors,
filthy ovens and happy kids.

Real Mothers know that dried playdough doesn't
come out of pile carpet.

Real Mothers don't want to know what the vacuum
just sucked up.

Real Mothers sometimes ask, "Why me?" and get their answer
when a little voice says, "Because I love you best."

Real Mothers know that a child's growth is not measured
by height or years or grade. It is marked by the progression
of Mama to Mommy to Mom

Author Unknown

Chapter Eight

Mothers don't keep hours. They're always open twenty-four hours a day.

Position Wanted???

JOB DESCRIPTION:

Long term team players needed for challenging permanent work in an often-chaotic environment.

Candidates must possess excellent communication and organizational skills and be willing to work various hours and be on call 24 hours a day.

Some overnight travel required including trips to primitive camping sites on rainy weekends and endless sports tournaments in faraway cities.

Travel expenses not reimbursed.
Extensive courier duties also required.

RESPONSIBILITIES:

Must possess the physical stamina of a pack mule and be able to go from 0 to 60 in three seconds flat in case, this time, the screams from the back yard are not just someone crying wolf. Must be willing to face stimulating technical challenges such as small gadget repair, mysteriously sluggish toilets, and stuck zippers. Must screen phone calls, maintain calendars, and coordinate production of multiple homework projects. Must have ability to plan and organize social gatherings for clients of all ages and mental outlooks. Must handle assembly and product safety testing of a half million cheap, plastic toys and battery operated devices. Must assume final, complete accountability for the quality of the end product. Responsibilities also include floor maintenance and janitorial work throughout the facility.

EXPERIENCE REQUIRED:

None. On-the-job training offered continually exhausting basis.

WAGES AND COMPENSATION: You pay them, offering frequent raises and bonuses. A balloon payment is due when they turn eighteen based on the assumption that college will help them become financially independent.

CALL 1-800-2BE-AMOM

A Mom's Life

Take your plate into the kitchen, please.

Take it downstairs when you go.

Don't leave it there, take it upstairs.

Is that yours?

Don't hit your brother.

I'm talking to you.

Just a minute, please, can't you see I'm talking?

I said, Don't interrupt.

Did you brush your teeth?

What are you doing out of bed?

Go back to bed.

You can't watch in the afternoon.

What do you mean, there's nothing to do?

Go outside.

Read a book.

Turn it down.

Get off the phone.

Tell your friend, you'll call her back.

Right now!

Hello. No, she's not home.

She's still not home.

She'll call you when she gets home.

Take a jacket. Take a sweater.

Take one, anyway.

Someone left his shoes in front of the TV.

Get the toys out of the hall. Get the toys out of the bathtub.

Get the toys off the stairs.

Do you realize that could kill someone?

Hurry up.

Hurry up. Everyone's waiting.

I'll count to ten and then we're going without you.

Did you go to the bathroom?

If you don't go, you're not going.

I mean it.

Why didn't you go before you left?

Can you hold it?

What's going on back there?

Stop it.

I said, Stop it!

I don't want to hear about it.

Stop it, or I'm taking you home right now.

That's it. We're going home.

Give me a kiss.

I need a hug.

Make your bed.

Clean up your room.

Set the table.

I need you to set the table!

Don't tell me it's not your turn.

Please move your chair into the table.

Sit up.

Just try a little. You don't have to eat
the whole thing.

Stop playing and eat.

Would you watch what you're doing?

Move your glass, it's too close to the edge.

Watch it!

More, what?

More, please. That's better.

Just eat one bite of salad.

You don't always get what you want. That's life.

Don't argue with me.

I'm not discussing this anymore.

Go to your room.

No, ten minutes are not up.

One more minute.

How many times have I told you, don't do that.

Where did the cookies go?

Eat the old fruit before you eat the new fruit.

I'm not giving you mushrooms.

I've taken all the mushrooms out.

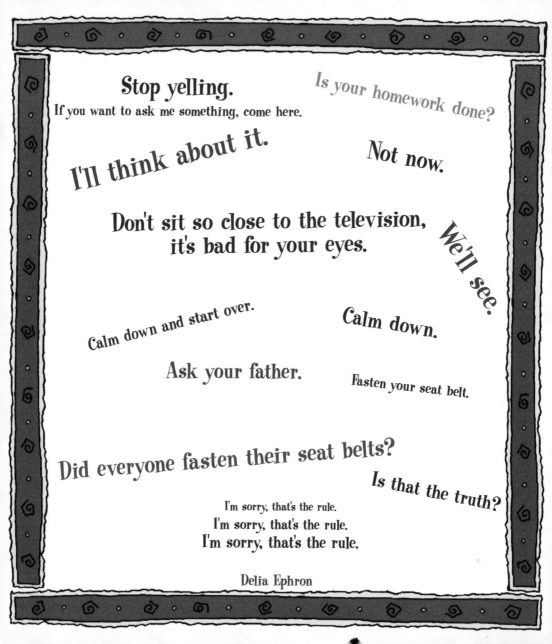

Stop yelling.
If you want to ask me something, come here.
Is your homework done?
I'll think about it.
Not now.
Don't sit so close to the television,
it's bad for your eyes.
We'll see.
Calm down and start over.
Calm down.
Ask your father.
Fasten your seat belt.
Did everyone fasten their seat belts?
Is that the truth?
I'm sorry, that's the rule.
I'm sorry, that's the rule.
I'm sorry, that's the rule.

Delia Ephron

If we laugh a lot,
when we get older
our wrinkles will all be
in the right places.

Anonymous

As for me and my house,
we will serve the Lord

Joshua 24:15

A mother's life is easier than you think.
All she has to do is:
Accept the impossible,
Bear the intolerable,
And be able to smile at anything.

Source Unknown

A mother is someone who...

- Insists you wear a sweater because she is cold.
- Makes you put on a scarf, hat, mittens, galoshes, and heavy coat at the first hint of winter.
- Will listen to the throes of a first love without giving advice.
- Thinks that her children are the cutest, the smartest, and the most creative.
- Will have chocolate chip cookies ready for you after your first day at school.
- Doesn't mind all the gerbils, snakes, lizards, dogs, and cats because she knows that a well-rounded child needs animals.
- Keeps your room just the way you left it when you go off to college.
- Will put up with a teenager's strange behavior because she knows that in time it will pass.
- Understands when no one else does.
- Tries to put your world back together when it is falling apart.
- A mother is love!

Rhonda S. Hogan

Children aren't ever sure what they want, but that's not the point - it's that they want it NOW.

E. Costello

All mothers are physically handicapped.

They have only two hands.

Anonymous

If it was going to be easy to rear children, it never would have started with something called "labor."

Anonymous

To become a mother is not hard. To be a mother is.

Rhonda S. Hogan

People who say they sleep like a baby usually don't have one.

Chapter Nine

Mother Won't Let Me

A policeman noticed a boy with a lot
of stuff packed on his back riding a tricycle
around and around the block.
Finally he asked him where he was going.
"I'm running away from home,"
the boy said.
The policeman then asked him,
"Why do you keep going around
and around the block?"
The boy answered,
"My mother won't let me cross the street."

A HAPPY FAMILY

A little girl once asked her mother:
"If Daddy can't get all his work finished at the office,
why don't they put him in a slower group?"
Anonymous

Let parents bequeath to their children not riches,
but the spirit of reverence.
Plato

Good family life is never an accident
but always an achievement by those who share it.
James H. S. Bossard

A happy family is heaven on earth.
Russian Proverb

Chapter Ten

Keeping Up With the Wyszynski's

As young newlyweds, life was hard.
Like a lot of other young couples,
my husband and I fell into the trap
of trying to keep up with the lifestyles
of our friends and neighbors. To make
matters worse, a new family moved
next door - the Wyszynski's.
You guessed it.
Now, not only were we trying to keep up
with their taste for fine things,
we had trouble just
pronouncing their name.

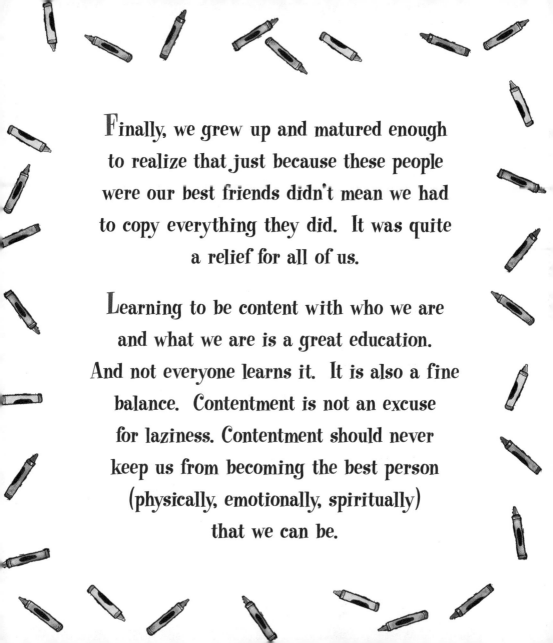

Finally, we grew up and matured enough to realize that just because these people were our best friends didn't mean we had to copy everything they did. It was quite a relief for all of us.

Learning to be content with who we are and what we are is a great education. And not everyone learns it. It is also a fine balance. Contentment is not an excuse for laziness. Contentment should never keep us from becoming the best person (physically, emotionally, spiritually) that we can be.

Contentment is an inexhaustible treasure.

Ancient Proverb

It is right to be contented with what we have, never with what we are.

MacKintosh

Contentment is the philosopher's stone that turns all it touches into gold.

Proverb

To have what we want is riches; but to be able to do without is power.

George MacDonald

Chapter Eleven

A MOTHER'S HEART

Hardening of the heart ages people more quickly than hardening of the arteries.

Anonymous

The heart has no secret which our conduct does not reveal.

French Proverb

To understand any living thing you must creep within and feel the beating of its heart.

W. Macneile Dixon

You can't reason with your heart; it has its own laws, and thumps about things which the intellect scorns.

Mark Twain

Delight yourself in the Lord and he will give you the desires of your heart.

Psalm 37:4

To be blind in the eye is better than to be blind in the heart.

Arabian Proverb

I have learned the secret of being content in any and every situation.

Philippians 4:12

He who wants little always has enough.

Johann Georg Zimmerman

God's voice speaks to the listening heart.

Two things are bad for people – running upstairs
and running down people.
Anonymous

The door to the human heart can be opened
only from the inside.
Anonymous

The clearest evidence that God's grace is at work in
our hearts is that we do not get into panics.
Oswald Chambers

Have a heart that never hardens, and a temper that
never tires, and a touch that never hurts.
Charles Dickens